Judith
Letting
Go

Judith Letting Go

Six Months in the
World's Smallest
Death Café

Mark Dowie

NEW VILLAGE PRESS • NEW YORK

Published in the United States by New Village Press
bookorders@newvillagepress.net
www.newvillagepress.org
New Village Press is a public-benefit, nonprofit publisher
Distributed by NYU Press

First Edition: February 2024
Paperback ISBN: 978-1-61332-235-2
Hardcover ISBN: 978-1-61332-236-9
eBook ISBN: 978-1-61332-237-6

Library of Congress Control Number: 2023948117

Cover illustration: SaraMarie Bottaro, *Night Blooming*,
acrylic on canvas, 2021

For

Peter, Sara,
and
Daniel

CONTENTS

"A Terrible Beauty Is Born"

For the entire six months I began to discover and understand Judith Tannenbaum, we both knew she was going to die. In fact, for most of that time we knew the exact hour she would go, sometime between 11:00 A.M. and noon on December 5, 2019, which she did. Although we knew each other only for those few short months, I will regard her for the rest of my days as a lifelong friend.

We talked about many things during those months, but the rapidly approaching moment of Judith's death came to inform and shape our entire conversation. Death was, as she put it, "the undercurrent and the overstory" of our relationship . . . one of the deepest, most profound, and fulfilling of my life. I'm not a great conversationalist. But Judith was.

While imminent death was really the only constant factor in our friendship, at no time during the months I knew her could Judith be described as "dying." In fact, she didn't want to be described that way. And until her last day, she wished to remain the vibrant, energetic, humorous, and life-loving woman she'd been for most of her life, and to be a lyrical poet, who wrote and revised her verse until the end, rarely mentioning her affliction to anyone, and only abstrusely in her verse.

Judith Tannenbaum hid excruciating pain from all but her family and intimate friends, and constantly sought ways to make life worth living in the face of agony, and then of death. To me, she was a paragon of courage, who, as her final day approached, reminded us all many times that she was not dying . . . "just letting go."

So, as a tribute to her life, and her courage, our story should not be read as yet another book about dying, or death and dying. It's about letting go of everything that matters to the living—attachments, hopes, plans, fears, and expectations—in preparation for the ending that awaits us all. And it's about how one person can expand another's compassion for anyone in pain.

The day before she left, I asked Judith if one day I could write about our friendship . . . for publication. Without hesitation, she said yes. Then I asked if there was anything we had said or written to each other that she would like me to leave out. I was surprised, but pleased, when she said no. So, except for what I might have forgotten, it's all here.

I then asked Judith's daughter and only child, Sara Press, to read an early draft of the manuscript, inviting her to change or remove anything that bothered her. Nothing did. So thank you, dearest Sara, for adding to the privilege your mother gave me by allowing me to tell our story.

And thanks also to friends and others who read and commented on the narrative: David Talbot, Doris Ober, Kate Dougherty, Jaune Evans, Suzanne Speh, B. J. Miller, my wise and supportive New Village editor Lynne Elizabeth, and the brilliant audio documentarian Robin Gianattassio Malle, who saw in the manuscript a potential podcast, on which we worked together for a few months but, for reasons unforeseen, have been unable to finish.

And Wendy, my beloved, I know this special experience of mine wasn't always easy for you to watch. But you did, and I know you understand now what Judith and I were doing, and can clearly see the value, hopefully to you as well as me.

CHAPTER 1

The Art of Letting Go

In the face of mortality, every decision takes
on a different meaning
—PAUL KALANITHI

Judith and I were introduced by a mutual friend, Kate Dougherty, who had known us both for years and was troubled by the way Judith was intending to end her life—not the fact that she was going to end it, but the way. Judith was about to book a flight to Zurich, Kate told me, with her only child, Sara. There someone from an organization called Dignitas would pick them up at the airport, take both to a sterile room somewhere downtown, and for almost eleven thousand dollars serve Judith a lethal cocktail. There Kate's closest friend would be, in a strange city miles from home, lying dead beside the person she loved most in the world, in a room rented by a death-for-hire association whose slogan is "To live with dignity, To die with dignity."

Surely, Kate believed, there must be a more dignified way to go. She called me because she'd heard that I'd helped people in Judith's straits. And she'd heard right. In fact, I had done so a few times, but never for anyone quite like this, someone who would change my life forever, and for the better, and mostly, though not entirely, because in the months to follow Judith Tannenbaum would teach me how to die. It was an ironic twist of fate because I had for some time been doing that very thing for others. Or at least I thought so.

During the fourth quarter of my life, as friends around the world began to face the end, I found myself spending more and more time helping some of them find a way out, all while lobbying quietly for legislation in my home state, California, that would allow *physicians* to do what I was doing—hasten the death of terminally ill people . . . people like Judith, who might not have been terminal but were living in pain that could not be medically treated.

I have to stop for a moment and make clear right now that Judith was not about to commit suicide. Neither Kate nor, eventually, I believed so. This may seem a bit strange at first, but I believe you'll understand us before the story ends.

As I promised Kate I would, I called Judith and arranged to meet and talk about her plan and her pain. And because it was at Kate's request, Judith invited me right over to her home.

And so began one of the deepest, most fulfilling friendships of my life.

*   *   *

Judith lived in El Cerrito, a blue-collar town of 25,000, three communities north of Berkeley, one east of Richmond, California. The first time I drove to her place, I thought she'd given me the wrong address. I had arrived, it seemed, at one of those quaint 1950s midwestern motels—a parking area up against a small lawn surrounded by half a dozen adjoining units behind enumerated pale green metal doors. Behind each door I imagined cookie-cutter interior about the size of a generous motel suite—bed, bath, kitchenette, and sitting area. I was not far off.

It wasn't a poet's loft or garret, really. But Judith had made it a poet's place . . . living simply, with plants in every corner, books open on the floor, and the constant aroma of strong tea. Every time I visited her, I would barely touch the bell at number 6 and the door would open, and there would be tiny Judith, beaming in black pajamas.

"As a young girl, I was shy," she told me the first day, "profoundly shy. I always sat in the back of classrooms, preferably behind one tall boy, a basketball player, so I couldn't be seen." If there was any residual shyness left in her, I never saw it. I asked her if she had overcome it. "I'm not shy when I'm comfortable" was all she said. And I became comfortable.

Unless she, or someone like Kate had told you, you wouldn't know that Judith had a severe, incurable form of an intractably painful neurological condition called Foraminal Stenosis, a restriction of the narrow vertebral bone passages through which most spinal nerves extend into the body. She described the pain to me in many ways, using a variety of words, all of which added up to *debilitating*. Strange as it may seem, she never showed signs of pain until one day, fairly early in our friendship, while we were chatting casually in her living room, she dove suddenly onto the floor, apologizing profusely, then explained that lying flat on a hard surface was the only way she had found to bring some relief from the sudden shocking pains that often accompany spinal stenosis. This was not a pinched nerve. It looked more like a half dozen or so nerves, all being pinched at once. Agony.

Judith spent a lot of her time alone on that floor, she told me, "mostly listening to music and reading poetry," and gritting her teeth, as she was at that moment. As she lay there, as slender and fit as any athlete I'd known, staring at the ceiling, again in black pajamas, we bantered for a while about how difficult it was, even for trained wordsmiths like ourselves, to describe pain in terms other than adjectives that could also be used to describe storms and economic collapse.

As she lay there, I began to wonder if pain like hers could actually kill a human being. If I was going to help Judith make the right decision, I needed to know the answer to that question. I asked some experts. The long answer seems to be yes, pain can kill, but not by itself.

Pain kills indirectly by setting off a cascade of separate anatomical crises that can end in death. The most common scenario seems to begin when a sharp and sudden pain sends an organism into shock, which leads either to a complete breakdown of the immune system or a stroke or cardiac arrest—conditions often listed as a "proximate cause of death."

So was Judith's affliction—severe foraminal stenosis—a "terminal" condition, a "proximate cause of death"? By itself, probably not, which may explain why I found only one medical journal that used the word *terminal* in describing foraminal stenosis, and did so cautiously, stating that only the most severe cases could be regarded as life-threatening. But it certainly seemed to me at the time, having watched Judith experience more than one attack, that her pain could lead to dire results.

But I will wonder for the rest of my life whether or not physical pain justifies death. I suppose the only pain we can truly understand is our own.

Judith's decision to end her life was not sudden, rash, or impetuous. She had been in worsening, debilitating pain for years, and mulling over ways to end her existence long before we met, all while trying every pain clinic, specialist, treatment, drug, and prosthesis she could find. Eventually, nothing worked, and in her words, "My body simply can't carry this pain anymore. There's not enough room for it."

She *was* petite, slight, *and* reflexively poetic . . . a published poet, in fact, who challenged the myth held by many that poetry really can't be taught. Rejecting that notion, she shared her talent with children in Mendocino elementary schools, later with lifers in California's San Quentin State Prison, and eventually with me. She had come to regard the teaching of poetry as her life's work.

"Poetry gives life meaning," she said one day, "particularly verse that rises from the imagination and the heart at once." By teaching students how to turn thought into words, and words into thought, Judith gave meaning to the lives of small children, many of whom still write poetry, and large men like myself and Spoon Jackson, an African American from Mojave, California, locked in San Quentin prison for life at twenty, believing that his existence had lost all meaning . . . until one day he strolled into a classroom and sat quietly in the corner to see if it might be a course worth taking. The teacher was Judith, who invited Spoon to join the class, then taught him to turn a prosaic life into verse. More on Spoon to come.

*   *   *

At first, "There isn't room in my body for this pain" seemed to me like an oversimplified and rather inadequate reason to die. But as time wore on and I watched her reacting to her affliction, I realized that while most pain is controllable, some is not (mild spinal stenosis is treatable; severe is not). I began to understand her choice, which had been made, I realized, after a long and thorough deliberative process, during which sheer agony gradually overrode the meaning and purpose of her life. But I was also haunted at times by the observation of a seasoned psychotherapist I have known and respected for years, who, when I asked his advice, simply said, "Pain can drive people mad."

Pain can drive people mad. Hmm. When I heard him say it, it sounded a bit simplistic, but as I watched Judith suffer in the months that followed, I came to believe that he wasn't completely wrong. Perhaps if not mad, pain can drive people to desperation . . . and of course desperation can sometimes look like madness.

While I eventually supported her decision to let go, and never thought Judith was mad, I still questioned the way she was planning to end it, and expressed my sentiments in an email:

> To my mind traveling to Switzerland with your only child and paying someone to end your life there is tantamount to "suicide," which we have agreed not to call this, although Dignitas, which lists as one of its eight stated purposes "suicide and suicide attempt prevention," will call it almost anything else to soften the blow and escape the global stigma of "assisted suicide."
>
> And do you really want or need to fly 6,000 miles and meet an alleged "doctor," who you've never met, whose third or fourth language is English, in a sterile, artless room, and pay him $11,000 to do what he does all day and serve you a shot of Nembutal (pentobarbital), which, if you can't get a prescription for it, you can find here, through

channels, for a few hundred dollars, and take in your own bedroom, with loved ones encircling you? That's exactly what you would do in some impersonal motel room in Zurich . . . then pay a lot more money to have your body cremated there, or, worse, flown back to California in a cargo hold of a 747 for burial . . . with Sara upstairs grieving in coach.

I'm sorry to be so graphic, Judith, and somewhat negative about the Swiss option, but I do want you to consider all possibilities before deciding what's best for you. In that vein, I assume you will have examined and considered every medical option for living with your affliction before you choose to end your life.

And if after doing that you remain set on dying soon, I suggest you seek the counsel of people and organizations that specialize in offering end-of-life advice and guidance. I will steer you to them if you ask. I just hope you won't make a final decision before you have explored every option and spoken to everyone who loves and cares for you. I'm sure you won't. But sometimes these things need to be said.

I expected Judith would respond directly to my advice, and tell me more about how pain had driven her to opt out and die on her own terms. Instead, she wrote this:

My first thought when I understood I was facing extreme pain and limitation for a very long time was of my mother who just turned 100. She is blind, bed-bound and unable to do almost anything for herself. I've had primary responsibility for her for the past 20 years and seen up close what it means physically, emotionally, financially, and in terms of dependence to live a very long life. This is a big part of what's brought me to my decision.

I can tell you more about my thinking— values and choices—if you want, hoping you'll feel comfortable giving me leads— specific if possible, more general if not. I'm

not at the point of ending things immediately, I just want to keep all options open.
And I hope you can help me do that.

What stayed with me from that note—in fact,
haunted me for the next six months—was the part
about her mother. I simply couldn't stop wondering how a very old woman would respond to her
daughter's death, no matter what she was told, or
how she heard the news. But I kept quiet about it
for a while.

"The essential point," I responded, "is that you
are doing everything right. You're not rushing;
you're exploring every option; you're talking to
everyone that matters; and you're seeking counsel;
I hope you are meditating as well, and that for as
long as possible, you will remain open to every
conceivable option . . . including life."

"Thanks so much for assuring me I'm doing
this right," Judith replied. "It's been so hard to
think straight through all this pain and to keep
everything important in mind . . . not only what I
want for myself but for Sara and my friends, and
how to protect them as best I can. You know I
might have figured things out on my own, very

slowly, but you've suddenly become my primary wise one and I can never adequately express how grateful I am." In the months to follow, I came to realize that gratitude was Judith's anchor . . . and forgiveness her practice.

But I began to wonder, as I had so often, about the ethical quandaries of helping someone die. The arguments against doing what I was doing, even those inspired and dictated by excessively powerful and dogmatic, mostly religious, institutions, can be compelling, but really only if there is some sort of payoff for the helping survivor—an inheritance, a reduction in expense, or simply the riddance of an obnoxious old relative. The answer is in the motive, and none of those motives applied here.

So was I doing this for love? I wondered. Partly, I supposed, as I did love Judith, still do. Or was it compassion for the dying? Not really. In truth, it was more selfish than that. I was training for my own endgame. And I had found, if not a coach, a willing and deeply beautiful exemplar.

*   *   *

During the months that followed, Judith and I stayed pretty much in constant touch, mostly by email, two or three exchanges a day. There were also long phone calls and conversations over tea in Judith's tiny apartment, where we talked for hours about impermanence, surrender, detachment, transience, grief, entropy, afterlife—if perchance it exists—and the fine art of meditating on death; Judith, as always, in black pajamas.

And of course we discussed poetry, the ultimate form of wordsmithing, all the while laughing out loud at the dodgy, poetic words and phrases we had both picked up during our lives to avoid the horrifying *d* and *s* words—*d* for *death*, my favorite euphemism for which is "crossing over," followed closely by "passing on" and "transitioning"; and *s* for *suicide,* a semantically tortured and deeply misunderstood word that we agreed should not be used to describe Judith's path, real suicide more often being the impetuous act of a depressed or overanxious person, something that too often ends a life that could and should have continued.

Judith recalled and could recite in detail the despondent lives of female poets who had opted out of life early—Sylvia Plath, Virginia Woolf, Anne Sexton, Elise Cowan—writers whose work she loved and admired but whose lives she didn't envy. Yes, she understood the close and sometimes productive relationship between depression and creativity, and clearly believed that pain could be turned into art, but she "could identify with none of the poets" whose despair had lead to suicide.

While I knew her, Judith never showed a hint of depression or anxiety, although she said she'd experienced both earlier in her life. Hope for an end to excruciating physical pain had simply abandoned her and she just wanted to get away from it. It was pain, not despair, that was stifling her creativity and wrecking her life. Around that reality Judith created new ways to communicate a decision that often troubles family and friends.

Rarely is death by suicide preannounced and carefully planned in advance like this, she observed, and even more rarely for six months, with a precise hour of departure entered in the calendars of everyone who mattered. The suicides we both knew were sudden, impulsive, and shocking. They were suicides, and this was something else.

The precise wording of our project remained a semantic obsession. Was "hastening my death" the same as "taking my life"? Was gradually "letting go" really any less proactive than jumping from a bridge? And why, we wondered together, was *suicide* stigmatized by being attached to the word *commit,* as if voluntarily ending one's life was somehow a crime?*

At the same time as we avoided words that made us uncomfortable, we sought a vocabulary that made sense of mortality, and explored ways that someone facing death could define herself. In that vein, we both took comfort in the articulate counsel of writers who had covered the subject: Carlos Castenada, Elisabeth Kübler-Ross, Philippe Ariès, Frank Ostaseski, Sara Davidson, B. J. Miller, and Katy Butler. But ultimately we agreed to favor the counsel of a Yale University professor of medicine named David Katz. Dr. Katz reminds us that "we do not own life, we wear it for a while. It doesn't belong to us; it flows through us. Death is no more

---

* Suicide has been considered a crime in many societies and still is in twenty-five nations. Attempting suicide is a serious misdemeanor in many more. It was not decriminalized in the United Kingdom until 1961. Early Greeks and Romans thought it was okay as long as you weren't a slave or a soldier. As a slave, your life belonged to your master; as a soldier, to your country. You therefore had no right to take it. Of course, there were not many ways your master or commanding officer could do to punish you if you succeeded.

enemy to us than autumn is to summer; it's what happens next . . . the common end to every story."

"The common end to every story." Of course Judith loved that.

"Pain and suffering," Katz says, "is our true enemy." And how could Judith not agree with that? Of course it took us back to semantics. "We can work on better wording," she said.

We tried "ending it all" and a few other evasive euphemisms before settling on Derek Humphrey's "self-deliverance," but that only worked for a while, and we ended up with Judith's simple "letting go," which we agreed best described her process—one by one releasing all the possessions, memories, emotional burdens, and insignificant acquaintances accumulated, item by item, person by person, and fear by fear, the things we that we all hold on to as we cling desperately to our existence, as if they and our existence are somehow interminable.

"Life is hard" Judith would say, "but death is harder." I had never met anyone, and probably never will, who was so comfortable talking about death, particularly about her own. It was as if we were discussing gardening, cooking, or training a pet. The "Life Reaper," as she called him once, became a third party in our conversation, always present, mostly silent, strangely cordial, at times a friend, and of course throughout, our "wise advisor" and "secret teacher."*

But as we talked, wherever and whenever we did, I couldn't stop thinking about her invalid mother, for whom Judith still described herself as "primary caretaker." "I don't know her, of course," I wrote, "but I do recall you telling me that despite her age she is quite alert to what's happening and still enjoys being alive? To tell you how I would respond to hearing that one of my children was planning to opt out of life would be a senseless projection. But I can't help imagining that it would be a serious shock for anyone who was sane and conscious . . . a possible life-wrecker. Have you

---

* *Wise Advisor* is a term borrowed from Carlos Castaneda, who believed that the main challenge of life was to "balance the terror with the wonder of being alive" and, in maintaining that balance, to see "death as the only wise advisor we have." Death was also a constant reminder "to be alert," "a reference point to behave with kindness," and "a shaking off of pettiness and daily concerns. . . . The worst thing that can happen to you," Casteneda said of death, "is already happening." *Secret teacher* is Frank Ostaseski's term for death. Ostaseski is cofounder of the Zen Hospice Project in San Francisco.

discussed anything about you plan with her? With your sister, your daughter, your therapist? That seems like an essential step in your deliberative process. But of course it's also your process, your life and your business."

Right after I sent that message, I wondered if I had been too harsh, too forceful. But she answered immediately:

You do have a way of asking tough but essential questions, Marko, and your timing is perfect. The question you raise haunts me day and night. What if my mother's still alive when I'm about to go? What should I tell her? Despite her age her mind is ok, although she's very into herself and doesn't want to know much, especially about anything difficult to absorb. So we don't talk deep at all.

My provisional thought is to say nothing right now because she may die before I do. If she doesn't, and the time's getting close, I'd say something like "I have an illness related to all the pain and I'm likely to die of it soon." This half-lie is in fact what I'm telling many people in my life; the ones I'm not close enough with to tell the whole truth. I don't feel great about the deception because I'm so much more comfortable with total truth. But a half-lie still allows me to talk about my feelings approaching death.

In my mother's case I simply can't see how the whole truth would serve her, particularly when I'd have to tell her how watching her decline has influenced my choice. Nothing remotely good would be served by that. As you say, it would be a total life-wrecker.

Judith said later that she was "frankly more concerned about Sara than my mother."

So for a while I dropped the subject of her mother, whom I never met, but I have often wondered how she responded to hearing that Judith was gone. I'll never know, of course. She died not long after Judith. But having lost two children myself, I know there is no good way or time to hear that news. So I simply said, "It's not only a 'half-lie,' Judith, it's a half truth. According to some medical assessments, your condition can be lethal. One even describes it as potentially 'terminal.' So telling your mother that you are very close to the end was not truly a lie."

Judith then asked my permission to say something she thought might make me uncomfortable. "Judith, you can say anything you want," I said.

"So can you," she replied.

And that became our abiding contract.

*   *   *

Death is not something most of us just start talking about, or a subject we want to force on someone living with a serious illness, in pain, or even on people like myself, who are simply living in overtime. But watching Judith process her endgame ignited my curiosity about it, so early in our conversation I cautiously broached the idea of forming or joining a "Death Café,"* a few of which existed

---

* The Death Café was born in England in 2011, "to increase awareness of death with a view to helping people make the most of their finite lives." Since then, Death Cafés have become a worldwide movement where people, often strangers, gather occasionally to eat cake, drink tea, and discuss death, dying, and facing mortality. The idea spread quickly across Europe, North America, and Australasia. As we go to press there are almost sixteen thousand active Cafés in eighty-five countries.

within walking distance of Judith's home . . . and to her very last day alive, Judith loved to walk. We both knew people who would join us to take an hour or so of every week to discuss and gain control over the most significant event we ever have to face. Judith liked the idea but said, "Let's start small." By that, she meant the two of us.

"I already have death conversations," she said, "with close friends and family, like Sara, Karen, Maxim, Emma, Kate, and others. So those doors are open, which is a big relief. But your idea of a formal group conversation, intriguing as it may be, is something I simply don't have the stamina for right now. Also some of the literature you've given me warns against talking too much, relating stories of police being called by well-meaning people trying to stop something they think is wrong. So I'm trying to take that in as well. So much depends on what's ahead. I fear it's mostly days like today where I could do so little, particularly what I love, like walking."

That night I wrote back: "I do understand your not having the strength or inclination to dive into a formal or regular conversation about death. And I don't want to seem like I'm pushing the Café idea.

I'm not. You should do everything at your own pace. And I'm glad you have close and loving people with whom you can discuss things that are so hard for some people to even think about. So yes, let's start slow . . . as we already have. Then maybe you can invite Maxim and Karen over to talk about joining us . . . then maybe Kate, then Janet, even Sara. But do what feels right, Judith, and only expand your Café if you're up to it. And if you don't want me to be part of it, of course I'll understand. I love this conversation just as it is."

So there was a possibility that we might add a friend or two along the way and build our little Café's membership to the recommended six or seven, eight max. But for sheer lack of bandwidth, that never happened, and for the next five months Judith and I continued to share views on death, alone together, talking about everything connected to it, particularly life, and laughing often about being members of "the world's smallest Death Café."

Even without a larger formal meeting, Judith grew increasingly comfortable talking about death with more and more friends and family. But while she did so, I tried to be the one person in her life with whom she didn't have to discuss the normal subjects people seem to obsess over while approaching the end—wills, DNRs, funerals, mortuaries, and remains. Instead, we talked about fears, mostly the fear of not existing, regrets, hope for survivors, legacies, and our plans for existence in the Elysian Fields. That part provided the comic relief.

Incidentally, I have to give Judith credit for most of the hilarity in all our conversations. She was quick to see humor wherever it lurked. Her bright laughter was immediate. And to the very end, she never lost sight of the absurd.

Laughter doesn't come from nowhere, I know. It's generally preceded by something humorous. But one has to see the humor to laugh. Judith's sense of amusement was genuine, deep, and contagious. I never ceased to be amazed at how quickly someone in excruciating pain and so close to death could laugh out loud, and right up to her last day alive, which I'll tell you about when you know her better.

As we talked and talked about it, I began to wonder if there were any original thoughts about death . . . about anything, for that matter. Humans have been thinking and recording their thoughts about every imaginable topic for so many centuries—millennia, in fact—that it seems almost a mathematical certainty that true originality probably died sometime during the Dark Ages, perhaps earlier. And on a topic as widespread and ubiquitous as death, it's hard to find anything original.

Of course everything heard, seen, or discovered for the first time is, to its recipient, original. And during my time with Judith, I heard, saw, or read what seemed to be scores of original thoughts about death. That hasn't made me ready for it, as Judith certainly was on her final day. But it has prepared me to take a step into the darkness without losing my balance.

CHAPTER 2

Café Conversations

You can't sell life as okay when it's not.
—TOMMY ORANGE

Our Café exchanges often began with a question one of us would ask the other. One day, for example, Judith asked me how I would prefer to die. My first impulse was to recite a poem I had written years before about that very thing. At the time, I had been working for three decades or more as an investigative reporter, who had spoiled the lives of hundreds of people I still believe deserved to have had their lives spoiled. I called the poem "Death Wish of a Muckraker."

I hesitated to start my recital to Judith, sensing it might gross her out, as it had others, but I went

ahead and gave my favorite poetry teacher proof
that I was not a poet:

He gets what he deserves
But not until his work is finished
When a bullet
Fired by one
Whose evil
He's exposed
Splits a weary skull
Which bleeds out slowly
Staining forever
The assassin's
Priceless carpet

As I blurted out my sordid little death wish, I
watched Judith's face, fearing she would be horri-
fied by the scenario, and the blood. I should have
known by then that she would laugh out loud,
which I'm relieved to say she did. Then I told her
the truth.

I really want to die as my father did—ready to
go at ninety-two, suffering while he was still alive
from what I asked his doctor to place on his death

certificate after "Proximate Cause of Death": "Existential Exhaustion."

"I'm just tired of being, Marko," Dad told me a week or so before drifting off peacefully one night, "so please don't let them try to stop this. Just let me go. And don't get all upset about your ol' pappy dying. He's had a terrific life." That he did, and an enviable death. Of course I'll never know whether or not he truly understood what was happening to him, or if he stepped through that final door full of wonder. We never talked about that, or anything spiritual, for that matter. I'll never know if he believed in God or an afterlife. But that's okay; I don't really know either about myself.

Dr. Graham, who had been treating Dad for decades and knew him well, listened respectfully to my request, looked up at me for a second, smiled, and carefully printed "Existential Exhaustion" on a blank Ontario death certificate. "I can't sign it until he's gone," he said. "Things could change." Nothing did, and Graham signed it the morning after "ol' pappy" slipped away into the night.

"So, like my dad," I said to Judith, "I want to wear myself out, like an old draft horse I knew and loved named Sharif, who became so tired of standing alone in the pasture for ten years after his work was done that he just lay down slowly one night and let go. And incidentally, like Woody Allen, and I assume Sharif, I am not afraid of dying, but unlike Woody, I *do* want to be there when it happens."

I want to watch the lights dim and the whole show that follows, as cell by cell, neuron by neuron, organ by organ, flesh and bone become inert and useless, as eternal darkness and silence descend, synapses begin to misfire and, chapter by chapter, I release everything that is impermanent in my existence, ending with my being. Or as another too-young-to-die friend, Chris Hitchens, put it his elegiac final book, *Mortality,* "I want to be fully conscious and awake in order to 'do' death in the active and not the passive sense . . . and try to nurture that little flame of curiosity and defiance: willing to play out the string to the end and wishing to be spared nothing that properly belongs to a life span."*

---

* Christopher Hitchens, *Mortality* (New York: Twelve/ Hatchette Book Group, 2012), p. 58.

Others have inspired the same sentiment. "I'd like to be fully conscious of it all," Jules Renard wrote shortly before he died, in 1910, "because you know I'd just be missing out on something otherwise." And the ever ironic Julian Barnes quipped that he wouldn't mind watching himself die, "as long as I didn't end up dead afterwards."

Judith responded by saying she had stopped thinking about best ways to go after selecting the one she had chosen. "It might not be my ideal way out," she wrote. "But since I know I have no other choices, I don't really want to dwell on better ways to die. It's time to let go. I was just curious to know what you hoped for yourself." Then she added this: "Also wanted to tell you that in a break from pain late last night I was able to imagine the moment immediately before my death when all I really wanted to do was say thanks—to life, to this sad sorry body that's held my life, and to death itself. A big settled feeling came over me, a rightness, and a commitment to myself not to look back. I have you partly to thank for that." Through the ninety-four days that followed, I watched and listened carefully as Judith's ever-expanding gratitude became the compass that guided her to a soft landing.

And I began to wonder whether or not, at some level, we all seek to influence, if not control, our deaths. And if we wish for a perfect ending, why aren't we more proactive about arranging it? And why do we so rarely tell our closest friends and family how we'd like to die? We'll tell them what we would like them to do with our remains, but not how we choose to spend our closing moments. I suppose this is what Death Cafés are for. Although I am sorry now and surprised, in retrospect, that the question never came up in our tiny Café. But this one did: What does *future* mean when you no longer have one? I've forgotten who raised his name first, Judith or I, but Paul Kalanithi immediately came to mind.

A professionally agile young neurosurgeon with a family and promising career at Stanford, Kalanithi was diagnosed with lung cancer at thirty-six, and died a few months later, to the end full of promise and purpose. He died fighting death, in the middle of writing *When Breath Becomes Air*, a brilliant, poignant, and deservedly best-selling *mémoire de mourir*, finished after he'd gone by his widow, Lucy, while raising their daughter, Cady, born while her father was consciously letting go.

While the book is about life, love, medicine, marriage, and many other things, the central theme is about losing a future. At least that is what came through to both Judith and me as we read the memoir in tandem.

Although he was trained to combat death, Kalanithi "acted not as death's enemy," he wrote, "but as its ambassador."* He was what is known on some hospital wards as a "death talker." I know the term because my stepmother was one. When a patient on the cancer ward where she worked at Toronto General started talking about death, fellow health-care workers, particularly surgeons who seemed to be particularly uncomfortable around the subject, would ask "Nurse Barbara" to come to their patients' bedsides and have a chat with them. Barbara always knew what the chat was to be about, she being the only person on her ward who would talk death with patients or their families. She listened attentively, absorbing every fear they had in calm silence. And she would pray with

---

* Paul Kalanithi, *When Breath Becomes Air* (New York: Random House, 2016), p. 77.

them if they asked her to, and cry when they did. Something about mutual crying makes the subject of death easier for some people to approach and its darkness to endure.

Judith and I cried together only once. It started without prompt or evident reason, and in complete silence one afternoon after two or three hours of not so light conversation. Judith, resplendent in her pajamas, brought two steaming mugs of tea from the kitchen and sat down in front of me. As we sipped our tea, we just looked at each other, and in less than a minute we were both crying. We never took the time to trace the source of our tears—another item saved for a Café conversation that didn't happened. But I now believe I understand what *was* happening, at least to me. I was grieving.

Except for the last day of her life, which I'll recount later, and one or two more after she left, I have barely grieved for Judith. I miss her terribly at times, and will never forget her, but that paralyzing, soul-crushing agony described so graphically by Joan Didion after her sudden loss of her husband, John Gregory Dunne, and soon after that of their daughter, Quintana Roo Dunne,* and by so many other powerful writers, appears to have passed before Judith died, but only for me. I know that Sara; Shandy, Judith's son-in-law; Kate; Debbie, Judith's sister; her niece, Emma; and others who loved her deeply are feeling it still. All I can remember of it now is how strange it was to look at a living person and feel something I didn't expect to feel until she was gone.

Like so many other things about this friendship, it was defined by knowing exactly when it would end. And like so many other things about death itself, things about this one will remain a mystery. Part of the mystery was wondering if I had become too focused on "the experience" and not enough on Judith . . . or on what this entire project might be doing to my marriage.

Because my relationship with Judith was untrammeled by attachments, plans, secrets, fears of abandonment, and also free of complexity, commitment, duties, promises, and even the normative expectations of friendship, it became, as we both

---

* Joan Didion, *The Year of Magical Thinking* (New York: Knopf, 2005) and *Blue Nights* (New York: Knopf, 2011).

observed, "pure." I never thought before that there could actually be a relationship, a friendship that could be described as pure. But I was wrong, and here it was, kept so by the certainty and totality of its ending. We both knew, throughout, not only that it was going to end but also precisely when.

To others in our lives, particularly my wife, Wendy, it seemed at times "unfair ... too easy." And in a way, Wendy was right. It *was* easy. Despite the looming heartbreak and constant profundity of our story's inevitable ending, Judith and I were always comfortable together, and, due to our "contract," able to say things to each other that wouldn't have been possible had one of us not been facing death, or if we were in any way committed to each other, which we were not.

What made it even easier for both of us was the realization we shared, that under our circumstances we could also say things out loud that we couldn't comfortably say to anyone else in our lives. Alone together, talking mostly about death, we had no vulnerabilities, and Judith began to reveal herself in ways I'm sure she never would have under less terminal circumstances. We discussed matters that committed couples, even closely bonded friends, are wary of, and may only discuss under the guidance of therapy or mediation, things that in unfacilitated relationships crash up against vulnerabilities, insecurities, and abandonment anxiety, all of which Judith and I both had, of course, but not in *our* relationship, and not in ways or forms that could possibly wreck or ruin a terminal friendship. That was liberating.

But it was also troubling to Wendy, who at one point described my relationship to Judith as "a love affair." Although it lacked the usual indiscretions and infidelities of a conventional love affair— secrecy, sex, and illicit romance—it was, to be honest, a loving and extremely intimate relationship . . . an experience anyone would envy, as Wendy later said she did. In truth, absolutely nothing between Judith and me was illicit or hidden, from Wendy or anyone else. Moreover, from the first day of our commitment, over forty years earlier, Wendy had encouraged me to love other women, just not erotically, and perhaps not quite as much as I love her.

But Wendy knows that when two people start talking about things like death, and one of them is staring it in the face, some intimacy is unavoidable. And I hoped—and still hope—that she could see the huge advantages of not having a committed relationship with someone you love, when the absence of eros opens and expands the opportunity for spiritual intimacy, allowing you both to go deeper in some ways than you ever had with each other. As Spoon Jackson said of his own "deep-diving" relationship with Judith, "She allowed me to be my weird, cool self." Once promises of fidelity are made, exclusivity and possession begin to spoil the flow, and "deep diving" becomes unsafe, or worse, unfaithful.

I haven't forgotten my promise to introduce you to Spoon Jackson. He's worth the wait. But first, a tragic interruption.

CHAPTER 3

The Real Thing

*"No one commits suicide because
they want to die."*
"Then why do they do it?"
"Because they want to stop the pain."
—TIFFANIE DEBARTOLO

With a matter of days left in Judith's life, my oldest stepson, Daniel, ended his, deliberately and
violently. I don't believe I've ever known anyone
with more purpose, commitment, and outright
humanity. As a boy, he was a high-energy force of
nature, who grew into a fiercely loving husband
and father of two terrific children fresh out of college. An idealistic and committed community
leader, Dan had a huge heart, which grew much
larger when someone needed him, especially a

child. He connected with and cared deeply about children.

He earned nationwide honor in his field, education, by starting and running some of the most imaginative and successful nonprofit charter schools in the country, most of them still operating successfully throughout the nation's public school system. His most recent creation he called the OnePurpose School, the single purpose of which was to get inner-city children through college, not just *into* but *through* college, a bold experiment that will take a dozen or so more years to prove itself. Sadly, Daniel will never see the outcome, which he would have made happen. It could fail in the absence of his energy and direction . . . another element in the tragedy of suicide.

Daniel's death was preceded two years earlier by the less surprising but equally sad and shocking suicide of his younger brother Peter. They were very close, Pete and Dan, and talked often about their shared affliction—depression-anxiety disorder—to my mind the worst imaginable version of clinical depression. I didn't know them as well as adults as I did as children, so for me the loss was really of two vibrant, athletic, and very happy boys, who showed no signs of melancholy growing up. But as they aged, for some reason they both became severely depressed adults. We're not supposed to lose children, but if we do, one is enough.

When I told Judith about Daniel, she suggested I take a "sabbatical" from our friendship, and abandon our tiny Death Café. Even a short absence, she believed, "will help you grieve." I thought about it for a second or two and realized that being in communication with Judith was exactly where I needed to be. By then I valued our friendship and her gentle wisdom more than ever. We didn't need to talk about Daniel or Peter, as their lives and deaths were in the room, and everything else in that room made their disappearances easier to face. So we talked about rational versus irrational suicide, agreeing that neither Peter's death nor Daniel's was rational, but that ending a life afflicted with incurable physical pain made enough sense to be rational, in fact, as we had already agreed, not really suicide.

But as I drove home the night after that conversation, I had to ask myself how stark the difference really was between Daniel's death and Judith's.

There is a lot in common between them, but too much difference to call them the same thing. Daniel's choice *was* suicide . . . irrational perhaps, but suicide. No point fudging that one. And there are those I am sure who would reflexively called Judith's chosen ending suicide as well, even if she asked them not to use the *s* word if they were ever asked how she died. And I heard her make that very request to more than one person.

On the trip home that night, I began to wonder about the term *good death*. Is it an oxymoron? What's good about it? And how about *dying well*? Is that possible? There was a time, not so long ago, when I thought both those expressions were self-contradictory nonsense—that was until my next-door neighbor died.

When Virginia Brownback was well into her eighties, she was still traveling the world, writing books about it, and living fully. One night, Ginny stuffed a sleeping bag and three days' provisions into her backpack, intending to set out with her two daughters the next morning on a three-day and -night hike through the Ventana wilderness. That night, she ate a sumptuous dinner, listened to her favorite opera, went to sleep excited about her forthcoming adventure, and never woke up. Enough said?

We humans think and talk endlessly about improving our lives, but rarely about improving our deaths. Is a good death the capstone of a good life? Would what I was doing then, with Judith, earn me a "good death"? We spend most of our lives trying to make life better, through exercise, diet, learning, and trying as best we can to understand it all. Only when it's imminent do most of us ever think about making death better.

Because she really had to think about it, Judith did that for herself. And lucky me to have been party to the process. There are those who accept death but hold it in contempt, some even regarding it as "the human curse," as only humans appear to be conscious of it. And there are those for whom another person's death is an affirmation of the survivor's power.

I have no interest in or claims to such thoughts, but I still wonder if being the only species of the millions on Earth whose individual members are aware of their own mortality is a blessing or a curse. When I think of or watch animals living as if immortal, I come to believe that perhaps some ignorance really can be bliss, and wonder at times if it's really necessary for death to play a central role in life. With Judith's help, I began to get over that notion.

*   *   *

No matter what else we would say to each other, Judith and I developed a habit of exchanging a "Death Café insight" whenever possible—in fact, almost every day. Here was one from me, written after a long September containing a dozen or more memorial services, capped by my oldest child's tragic leap from the Golden Gate Bridge.

> Being surrounded by death, as I have been in recent days (perhaps it goes with my age) hasn't been an easy or particularly uplifting process. But I have to admit that it has helped me face and contend with the full force of my mortality. I imagine every death is a lesson from which we learn more about our own. But you, courageous one, are by far

the most inspiring how-to-die role model I've ever known. Your exemplary grace, patience, and equanimity will stay with me to the grave.

I should have known better, as I knew by then that Judith profoundly disliked being seen as perfect or in any way exceptional. "No one has ever pointed to me as a model of patience or equanimity," she said the next time we were together, "but I seem to possess these qualities more now than I ever thought I might. Honestly, and maybe sadly, I think it's because I know I don't have to live much longer."

"You mean you don't have much longer to live?"

"No, I meant what I said."

I paused to shift the subject.

"I know you're not perfect, Judith. You're human," I said. "But you are exceptional and very courageous."

To which she responded, "Am I really courageous? I never see myself that way, especially as I know the huge fear I have and how that fear has shaped me."

"Courage is standing up to fear, Judith," I said, "something you have mastered."

"I am so grateful that you're standing next to me right now," she replied.

I paused, looked out the window for a moment, and blurted out a question that would persist through our entire relationship: "Why are you cutting ten years off your life, Judith?"

"Because they will be dominated by pain and unavoidable misery. Why live them after a life full of laughter, love, and joy?"

Of course I understood, and never raised that sadness-driven question again, and it eventually drifted out of mind, until our next meeting, when Judith made a soul-shaking announcement.

The original date she had set for her death was February 13, 2020—her birthday. Over tea that afternoon she told me she had to reset the date she would die. Again she repeated what she had said earlier. "There simply isn't room for more pain in this little body," and added a list of horrors, which up to that point she had only mentioned to other friends—her inability to tie her shoes, open jars, and her need to rely on friends and neighbors for tiny tasks. On top of that, she was losing her balance more often and feared she would fall again and sustain an injury that would prevent her from following through on her plan. "It's come to a point where I'm no longer fighting pain," she said; "it's fighting me." So, she told me, she had moved her date of departure back to December 5.

She's rushing, I thought. But I couldn't say that. In fact, I couldn't speak. I had to leave. I was paralyzed, simply unable to absorb the thought of losing two whole months with Judith. I faked an incoming text message and left suddenly, only to collapse, awash in tears, on the front seat of my car.

Of course I could have stayed and broken down in front of her, as I already had a few days earlier. But I didn't want her to see me do so under those circumstances. She would have felt responsible for my misery. Or at least that was my fear at the moment.

*   *   *

For much of the time we were meeting, Judith was reading Richard Powers's *The Overstory* for the third time. She would quote and read passages aloud from it, and was so taken with the work that she wrote this letter to its author:

Dear Richard Powers,

I write with so much gratitude for *The Overstory*, which I read as soon as it came out and which I've re-read twice in the 18 months since. I've written to you thanking you for your previous books because I've so valued how you look at important subjects. This time, in addition to that kind of appreciation, I also thank you for how deeply *The Overstory* has affected my life.

I've been very ill this past year. This might sound overblown but it is absolutely true that *The Overstory* is one guide that's helping me approach the end of my life with the best possible spirit and attitude. I feel so much love and light, connection, interdependence. Feel all I can't know or understand. Feel so happy as memories flow through me and then so happy letting them go. Feel so grateful for my life and also so grateful for my death. My daughter and son-in-law also read and loved *The Overstory* and we refer to your book often.

For itself (its structure and story, its vision
and values—for how you say what we see
and feel but are less able to say) and for
what your book gives us now as we go
through this small personal experience
together and as we try to stand upright
amidst the huge planetary grief we all
share.

I wish I had the stamina to spell out all
the particulars of my gratitude. But I don't,
so, again, I say thank you.

Judith Tannenbaum

When I arrived one day, Judith came to the
door, beaming from ear to ear, this time in faded
green pajamas. Something wonderful had clearly
happened. "He wrote back," she said with delight,
and showed me Powers's response.

Dear Judith Tannenbaum,

I have never received a letter from a reader
that has meant more to me. Your words are

an encouragement and a reminder that I
hope to keep with me for whatever time I
myself have left. I think often of my own
death and about how I might preserve the
moments of inclusion, expansiveness, and
grace that are our only answer to mortality.
To know that others can find, as you have,
the spirit of interbeing at the heart of a
good life and a good death, and to think
that my own words have helped you along
the way will be the deepest kind of
consolation as I reach my own end.

To try to stand upright amid the huge
planetary grief: that is our challenge in
every hour now, isn't it? But life—if not
humanity—is so long and so resilient; if we
ally ourselves with that immense journey,
then time is with us and nothing ends when
we do.

I am trying to think of what I can wish
you, in your closing chapters, but it sounds as
if you have found most everything already.
May you hold on to it until the last, and may
memory, attention, and imagination keep

you infinite. Thank you for the gift that you
have given me.

Richard Powers

I was speechless. I choked up, pressed the letter to my heart, and said, "Frame it." She promised
she would. But I never saw it on her wall. What a
treasure.

As I reread that exchange now that she's gone,
I remember that Judith was, as I've always tried to
be, an inveterate "biophile" . . . a lover not only of
the life she'd been given, the life she created in
Sara, but of life itself. "'Life in itself is sufficient,'"
she said one day, quoting Castaneda.* So often in
our conversation she would repeat how glad she
was that her death, "the only wise advisor I have,"
would leave space for more life, and acknowledge
that life in a finite ecosystem like a planet could
only last, be bountiful and beautiful if death took
out old life, leaving leaving room for the new. She

---

* The full quote from Carlos Castaneda's *Viaggio a Ixtlan* is:
"Life in itself is sufficient, self-explanatory and complete."

knew and repeated more than once that "without death, life could not have happened."

Of course there is, and always will be, a vast distance between thinking about death in the abstract and about one's own. I supposed that would never change. But it did, in Judith. And I was watching closely as she realized and said, in so many ways, that letting her own life go was a gift to the planet she loved.

CHAPTER 4

The Plan

Let death be what takes us,
not lack of imagination.
—B. J. MILLER

Judith never stopped exploring ways to end her life, reading just about everything she could find that didn't involve flying to Switzerland. She eventually focused in on two American volunteer-based organizations offering advice and guidance on right-to-die issues and options.

First came Final Exit Network, a splinter from the legendary Hemlock Society, which was created in 1980 by Derek Humphry (author of the classic *Final Exit*, written after he helped his terminally ill wife hasten her death). The other, also a Hemlock spin-off, was Compassion & Choices (C&C). Both offer and counsel end-of-life options, but C&C is also a leading advocate and lobbyist for death-with-dignity laws, such as New Jersey's Aid in Dying for the Terminally Ill Act. This act was passed in 2019, after several previous attempts to get it through the state legislature had been stifled, mostly by Catholic bishops who stormed the New Jersey capitol, as they had in every state capitol each time a similar bill came up, and threatened to excommunicate any Catholic legislator who didn't oppose it.

After exploring every possible option, and there were more than those two to chose from, Judith opted to seek advice and guidance from Final Exit Network (FEN), a 501 (c) (3) nonprofit based in Florida that believes "a mentally competent person with intolerable suffering or pain has the right to end their life, choosing the timing and persons present, and free of any restrictions by the law, clergy, medical professionals, friends or relatives." FEN offers direct hands-on assistance with self-deliverance, sending trained "guides" directly to your home. A careful distinction is made between suicide and hastening an inevitable death. "This is no kind of suicide," a FEN lawyer told me during an interview about the organization and its services. And FEN does not provide assistance to everyone who seeks it.

Compassion & Choices is more conservative and reserved about assisting death. This advocacy group seems to favor and counsel what it calls VSED—voluntary stopping eating and drinking, also known more graphically as VSAD—voluntary starvation and dehydration, a slow process that for a strong, otherwise-healthy person like Judith could last two to three weeks—not a particularly uplifting thing for loved ones to watch. After a brief discussion of that option, Judith decided she wanted no part of it; sudden death was her choice.

Prior to meeting Judith, those at FEN told her they had never regarded chronic or intractable pain as a qualifying rationale for their assistance. She had her work cut out for her. I had intersected with guides from FEN, so I had a sense of how they thought and worked. "Before they will accept your case," I told her, "they have to be convinced that you're close to death. And they are very good at assuring themselves that you are not simply some-one looking for assistance with suicide. They don't do that.

"Intractable pain, they know and understand, can be impossible to live with. But they also believe that depression and anxiety can be treated with medicines. So they will explore and want to see solid evidence of pain and futility ... and an absence of depression. They may ask for close witnesses—not people like me who know and sympathize with you, but people who have heard you scream, literally or figuratively ... your doctors, your neighbors, and your family. And they will ask to see your medical records."

After hearing her story firsthand and examining her well-organized and voluminous medical file, which contained reports and analyses signed by a dozen or more doctors and pain clinicians who had treated her over the years she suffered from severe foraminal stenosis, FEN guides and lawyers made their first exception and agreed to work with someone in pain—at a safe distance, of course.

Judith had learned from me and legal counsel that the less she relied on assistance, the less vulnerable others would be to criminal prosecution. FEN and several of its guides, who in some instances do operate at the margins of some state laws, had already been defendants in three criminal prosecutions—in Arizona, Minnesota, and Georgia. So she met two guides, listened carefully to their counsel, read Humphry's book and everything else she could find about self-deliverance, then, on her own, drove to an *Airgas* outlet and bought a canister of nitrogen. Also on her own she purchased the necessary attachments—tubing, release valve, and other paraphernalia—assembled and rehearsed the procedure she'd studied, and awaited the day she had chosen to "fly into the flame," with assistance from no one, most blessedly not from a stranger in Zurich.

As I watched Judith prepare alone for her own death, I began to wonder if Dr. Jack Kevorkian should be regarded as a hero of the right-to-die movement. He is by some, but I'm doubtful. To me, he seemed a narcissistic show-off whose portable, excessively complex Rube Goldberg killing machine was not very different from many states' execution chambers.

Everything Kevorkian did could have been done anonymously, simply, in silence, and without publicity. To me, his public killings defied the whole notion of "death with dignity" and stimulated a strong national opposition to what he claimed to be fighting for. I believe he set the movement for physician-assisted death back a decade or more. And I'm not alone in that assessment.

*   *   *

California Penal Code § 401 reads: "Every person who deliberately aids, or advises, or encourages another to commit suicide is guilty of a felony." There are similar statutes in twenty-four other states, all in criminal codes, all defined as felonies, and mostly punishable by imprisonment. I know of at least two living people, one male, one female, who have served time in California prisons, having been charged and convicted under that archaic law. These two cases were very different from each other, and bore no resemblance to anything I have ever done, or was doing with Judith. But Judith and I both knew, and acknowledged throughout our relationship, that even though I more than once tried to talk her out of ending her life, a strict interpretation of PC § 401 could land me in criminal court, perhaps in prison, although I do have a lawyer who knows what I've been up to and is prepared to defend me, pro bono. That's reassuring.

Judith took great care to protect me at all times, erasing any email exchanges that could be interpreted as advisory or encouraging, "which I suppose could mean *not* discouraging me to do this," she would say, chuckling. I reminded her that I had asked her early on if she had explored every alternative to her plan, which she had, and she had kept a record of every step in her process, indicating that everything she was about to do was at her own hand and her own volition. As part of her preparation, she drafted a personal letter, to be left next to where she would be found dead on her living room floor (the same place she often dived to in pain). It was addressed to the El Cerrito chief of police, whom she knew well enough to address by his first name.

Dear Chief Keith,

Today your officers will find my body. I've done this myself. No one helped, advised or encouraged me. I did all the research on the method, purchased the necessary equipment (receipts attached), prepared what I needed to prepare, and carried out the act alone.

After describing her affliction and detailing her carefully studied method of deliverance, she added this:

> I understand that you will probably have
> to label my act a " suicide." But suicide
> connotes mental distress, severe depression,
> loneliness etc and none of those apply to me
> in the slightest. I do this in a state of deep
> gratitude for life—life itself *and* the personal
> life I've been given. For all those whose love
> surrounds me I have made a rational choice.

A strict and legally literal prosecuting attorney might still regard me as a felon, because in the final analysis I didn't aggressively discourage Judith from ending her life. A strict interpretation of that fact, and Penal Code § 401, could be that I "encouraged" a suicide. Truth is, I would never encourage or assist a suicide. That is simply not what was happening here.

CHAPTER 5

Helping People Die

Do I really want to do this again?*

I had six months to adjust to Judith's decision, the first day of which was the easiest. We hadn't met yet. And when we did meet, for a while the basis of our relationship was strictly advisory. I was to guide her gently toward a sensible and graceful exit, something I had done enough times with others to be somewhat adjusted, even sanguine about the process, to a point where I could almost describe myself as a "death doula."†

---

* Note to self, 11/2/19. Days remaining in Judith's life: 33.

† *Doula* is the Greek word for midwife. Midwives (birth doulas) assist with the beginning of life; death doulas help with the end of it.

The problem this time was getting to know the departing person so deeply, and to gradually see the subtle but certain tragedy of someone like Judith leaving her life and the world this way. Unlike so many people I have known who ended his or her own life, including two children, Judith was not escaping depression, anxiety, failure, tragedy, a truly terminal illness, or a difficult existence. She was simply turning away from pain—chronic, intractable physical pain, not spiritual or psychological pain. This was one of the happiest, most fulfilled, and purposeful people I had ever met, anywhere. Her only curse was physical—pain that just wouldn't and could not be stopped.

*   *   *

This is as good a place as any to stop talking about Judith for a moment and tell you where I stand on self-deliverance and what she and I had been doing together. Back in the days before the title existed, I was executive producer of a small audio production company that created what are now called "podcasts," most of them for Public Radio Exchange (PRX) and SoundCloud. We called them "radio documentaries," "sonic blogs," or "audio docs" for short. Most of them were one-on-one interviews with authors or people who had just accomplished something special. None of these people was about to end his or her life. But one of my favorite projects was an hour-long documentary called *Helping a Loved One Die,* which focused on the very moral and ethical quandaries I would face twenty years later with Judith.*

While we were recording and editing the piece, my crew and I carried on a fairly fierce debate about what we were all calling "assisted suicide," although in the story itself we clearly differentiated between assisted suicide (aka "voluntary euthanasia") and hastening an inevitable death.

Like any good journalist, I tried to produce a fair and balanced report, not take a position during the research phase of the project, respectfully interviewing and including the voices of strong partisans on all sides of every question, and throughout the process remaining open and objective about what was at the time a raging controversy in the United States, particularly in California,

---

* As this book went to press, *Helping a Loved One Die* could still be heard on soundcloud.com by searching for the title or my name.

where I lived and worked. Only Oregon and Washington had at the time passed "death with dignity" or "right to die" laws, and the Montana Supreme Court had allowed physicians to assist terminal patients who wanted to hasten their death.

As we go to press, physician assistance in dying, under appropriately rigid guidelines, is now legal in ten U.S. jurisdictions—California, Colorado, the District of Columbia, Hawaii, Montana, Maine, New Jersey, Oregon, Vermont, and Washington— and eight other nations of the world. Legislation, referenda, and national court decisions all seem to be moving toward expansion of the right to die on one's own terms in twenty-four other U.S. states and several other countries around the world.

After listening respectfully to all sides of the debate, closely watching the decade-long legislative process that led to my state's passage of the End of Life Options Act in 2015,* and completing

---

* The End of Life Options Act was signed into law by then Governor Jerry Brown, a seminarian Catholic who I thought would never sign the bill. Well he did, but his signature didn't end my work, or my commitment to people like Judith, who don't quite qualify for physician-assisted death under the new statute, which to my mind doesn't go far enough, leaving

production of an hour-long podcast on the controversy, I come down cautiously on the side of allowing any person of sound mind to choose his or her moment and method of death, and, under dire circumstances, like Judith's, to ask for professional assistance, but of course only from a professional who approves of the practice. And having watched a friend, teacher, and brilliant poet suffer attacks of intractable pain, I believe that anyone in her condition has a right to end her or his life, and to seek a modicum of assistance in doing so. Without some guidance from an experienced friend or professional, it's just too easy to mess things up and leave a very sad scene for relatives and other survivors to try to cope with.

While journalists are trained to resist positions, orthodoxies, and isms, particularly on matters of high controversy, we get a little weak sometimes and opinions begin to creep into our all too human minds. In that vein, I confess to finding it strange—in fact, contradictory—that a culture that allows, supports, even worships individual

---

people like her and others I've known in constant, unbearable pain.

liberty, defends personal freedom, and encourages its citizens to "live and let live," would, in many of its jurisdictions, also deny them the right to die as they choose.

Death, I believe, belongs to the dying. And in the final analysis, that's all of us. Of course I respect people of faith who believe that only their God can make the final decision about when to end a life. That's their choice, based on their belief, but they have no right to make it mine or anyone else's. Nevertheless, many of them show up at legislative committee hearings, attempting to do that very thing.

Judith and I spent a lot of time discussing the values implicit in that debate, and in her choice. "Of course some things that matter do change . . . they have to," she said, "but not values . . . at least not mine. It took me years and many missteps to form and embrace them. Why should I change them just because I'm about to die?" During the six months I knew her, I never saw a value in Judith that needed changing.

CHAPTER 6

The Fire Drum

People are like stained-glass windows.
They sparkle and shine when the sun is out,
but when the darkness sets in, their
true beauty is revealed only if there
is a light from within.
—ELISABETH KÜBLER-ROSS

After I left Judith's place one cold day in early November, I passed a vacant lot nearby, a large open field of dust and stubble. In the center was a fifty-five gallon drum with a fire in it. Encircling the drum were a dozen or so mid- to late-in-life African American men. They were talking and laughing. I stopped, and then walked out to the circle.

Because I would soon be driving again, I declined their immediate offer of a beer, but I asked them if they knew a woman named Judith Tannenbaum, who lived three blocks away and frequently walked the neighborhood. They knew her, they said ... "Little Judy" ... and had read her poetry aloud in that very circle, from a book she had given them.

One poem remembered by name and loved by them all was called "Way Out in the Bay." It was about leaving San Quentin Prison, California's citadel of corrections, built on a small peninsula on the northwest shore of San Francisco Bay, where more than two of them had spent, as one said, "too much of our lives." None of them had a copy of the poem with him, but some remembered lines, which I scribbled down as they recited them: "This is the moment faultline / slide of two plates," "We're blind but we touch something whole," and "All I see is where we throw / what we don't want to look at."

I didn't tell them Judith was ailing, or that they'd probably never see her again. No reason, really. I just didn't have the heart to spoil their fun.

But when this book is published, I'll take some copies back to the fire circle and pass them around.

Anyone would be blessed to know someone who in a few months radically changed his values, and his very life . . . and both for the better. Even if only by her poetry, I sensed that Judith had some impact on most of the men around that drum. So we were all blessed to know her, I thought on the way home—privileged, in fact. And as I've come to know and hear from others in her life, I realize what a truly remarkable person we had all come to know.

WAY OUT IN THE BAY

Count's cleared and the guard says,
"It's late, class is over, you can go
back to your cells. Good night."

This is the moment faultline
slide of two plates.
Some shift I can feel
but not yet quite see.
This is the moment
dark screen descending.
This is the moment

cleave of an ax:
what came before and now this.

Before
      in that basement
buried room two flights down.
We're blind but we touch
something whole.
Call it poems.
Call it life.
Call it
we breathe
and we're human.

Now
      their way to the right.
The mural, barbed wire
North Block, Death Row.
Their walk in that dark
I can't see beyond.

And my turn to the left.
Past Four Post, the garden,
three chapels, three gates.
Outside to the car

where I sit frantic, desperate,
driven by light—
bridge lights and town lights
and stop lights and shop lights
and the light of the lamp
I've left on at home.

So much light and still
I can't see,
can't catch sight
of a shape
I might understand.
All I see are the stairs of a fortress
where light cut by grating
hits concrete in squares.
All I see is where we throw
what we don't want to look at.
Under low ceilings
way out in the bay.

One day I started writing a poem to Judith. My wife, Wendy, happened into my office when it was half written. I invited her to look over my shoulder and read what I had drafted. After skimming a few lines, she asked, "Are you in love?" I paused, thought for a few seconds, and said, "Yes . . . but not with Judith. I do love her, of course. You know that by now, but what I *am* in love with is this experience . . . getting to know a deep and wonderful person, whose beauty you've seen in person and in her writing, whose humor, compassion, and kindness are boundless, with whom I can discuss almost anything, even death and dying, openly and without fear or reservation. This is the most profound, liberating, and meaningful thing that has happened to me since I met and fell in love with you."

From the very beginning of my correspondence with Judith, Wendy was cc'd on all exchanges. About midway through our friendship, they met. It was a wonderful meeting to watch. "Two Jewish girls who love to laugh, meeting for the first time" is how Judith described it. I just sat back and watched. And was so glad to hear on the way home how much Wendy liked and admired Judith.

Eventually she saw how privileged I felt to share a short section of my life with someone who knew exactly when she was going to die . . . to befriend and witness someone truly letting go, who never showed a sign or symptom of existential anxiety as she quietly sought agency in her own death. This was an honor beyond imagination or belief. And that's what I was in love with.

CHAPTER 7

Spoon

To practice death is to practice freedom.
A man who has learned how to die has
unlearned how to be a slave.
—MICHEL DE MONTAIGNE

When we were together in her apartment, Judith was often lying flat on her back on the floor, almost always in pajamas. "It's the only place I'm comfortable," she said. One day the phone rang. She rose from her pain, cursed, and walked briskly over to the phone, mumbling something like "Another robo caller." She picked up the receiver and said, "Hello." Then she said, "Spoon," followed by a long silence as she listened intently to the last words she would hear from a friend of thirty years.

Spoon Jackson, an African American man from a tiny desert town in Southern California, is serving a life-without-parole sentence in New Folsom prison. Judith had taught him the art of writing poetry. She "believed in me even when she didn't know me," Spoon wrote of Judith in a memoir they shared of their friendship. He knew her plan and was calling to say good-bye. I couldn't hear what he said, but Judith was weeping as he offered his farewell. "I love you, too," she said, and hung up, returning to her position on the floor, where she lay on her back in silence, staring at the ceiling until she was ready to move on. I said nothing.

Spoon was one of a dozen or more prison inmates, most of them lifers, to sign up for Judith's poetry class, taught in the California Department of Corrections arts program at San Quentin. She was the first teacher in Spoon's life who wasn't wielding a paddle or length of garden hose with which to beat him. Through poetry, Judith revealed to Spoon a man who, he recalls, "did not believe that anything written by me was worthy, or anything inside was beautiful." Spoon Jackson's work is now published, and he is known throughout the California prison system as "the poet." And he's been nominated for poet laureate of California.

"I have been so incredibly lucky in my life," Judith said wistfully after the call. "The work I've been able to do...being present, with others opening up and sharing as much deep, painful beauty as they could manage."

All Judith seemed to want at that point was calm advice, simple human kindness, and a peaceful death. And that was really all I or anyone else could give her. But as we waited out the short time left till the end, she would give me so much more in return—a free course on dying. Death is the end of life, we know, but is it the end of existence? To a degree, I suppose it is...at least the existence of our bodies. But existence survives in memories, as Judith's will in mine.

On another phone call I overheard, Judith announced her decision to the caller, then remained silent throughout the rest of the call, said goodbye, and hung up. "Who was that?" I asked. "An old friend I haven't heard from in years. He cried and reminded me of a wonderful hike we took together years ago." She paused for a moment, lay back down on the floor, gazed out the window, and pondered the call.

"So this is how it unfolds," she said, sighing, "my whole life being given back to me in tiny chapters by friends who remember incidents I'd almost forgotten." She stopped, raised her head from the floor, and said with noticeable remorse, "Of course I'm going to have to stop rerunning their stories, one at a time, as I face the finish line. I guess that's part of letting go." Then she chuckled and added, "But I'll hold on to that one for a little while longer."

On my way out the door that afternoon, Judith dropped what was for me a loaded question to think about before our next meeting. It's one of the most frequently suggested meeting openers in Death Café advisory articles and instruction manuals.

"How do you want to be remembered?" she asked.

"Not too well," I replied.

She grabbed my arm and stopped me." What, exactly, do you mean by that?" she asked.

"Well, do you want to be remembered for *everything* you did?"

She paused for a moment, looked off to one side, and chuckled quietly.

"Good question," she said, and let me go.

Truth is, it really doesn't matter how I am remembered. I'll never know. I've been good to some people, less so to others. That's how I should and probably will be remembered; although fondly, I hope, by those I didn't offend or hurt.

When this book is published, it will be my tenth. To that, add somewhere around two hundred investigative reports, a bunch of op-eds, and a few turgid essays. But they are my legacy, not me. And their content has nothing to do with who I have been as a person, or how I should be remembered. I suppose I'll be remembered a thousand or more different ways, by the thousand or more people whose paths I've crossed.

The next time we met, I asked Judith the same question. She got up from the floor and went into her bedroom, the only other room in her house, and returned immediately with four personally signed books:

- *Disguised as a Poem: My Years Teaching Poetry at San Quentin* (a short memoir)

- *The World Saying Yes* (an anthology of her poems)
- *Carve This Body into Your Home* (another anthology of her work)
- *By Heart: Poetry, Prison, and Two Lives* (which I regard as her magnum opus)

By Heart is the powerful braided memoir of two lives—hers and Spoon Jackson's. To me, it's the heart of her legacy.

Those two lives could not have been more different. Judith, the well-educated, somewhat privileged daughter of a UCLA professor, and Spoon, the youngest son born of parents who tried and failed fifteen times to have a daughter.

Raised in a world of violence and neglect, Spoon was convicted of first-degree murder at twenty by an all-white jury, for killing a white woman. He doesn't deny the crime, only the circumstances. And he knows that were he not Black, he would not be serving life without parole. "Nothing to compare it to besides death," he wrote. "In prison I have learned to keep my laughter, smiles and feelings hidden behind a mask. And until I met Judith my heart was also hidden."

Reading Judith's side of the story, I began to realize that her active, purposeful, and compassionate life, more than anything else, helped her prepare to let go.

CHAPTER 8

Meditation

We best prepare for our final passage by allowing nature to guide us.
—RAM DAS

Judith and I both practiced some form of Buddhism, mine being less disciplined than her Zen, and leaning more toward Vipassana. This made our communication easier. We both understood the basics of right livelihood, impermanence, suffering, karma, detachment, etc., but most important, at least under the current circumstances, was our mutual appreciation of equanimity, a vital and ubiquitous aspect of the dharma, and ultimately an essential function for anyone facing death. And of course we both meditated.

Death meditation is practiced in all branches of Buddhism, and by mystics like the two of us. In one of our longer Death Café conversations, we compared meditations on death. Here they are:

Mine: Although I am spiritually inclined toward Buddhism, as you are, my death meditation is more Sufi (Muslim), as the focus is less on impermanence, or the end, or the circle of life than on the notion of surrender—gradual surrender.

So once a day, usually first thing in the morning, I attempt to unite my mind with nature, then, usually while exhaling a deep breath, I figuratively surrender my being, my entire being, to the creation of which it (my being, not my self) is a small and temporary expression . . . a gene expression. I then let my being float away until I am at peace with the eternal. Of course I return to commune with life for a while.

I love seeing death that way—proactive surrender—rather than having something taken from me . . . life . . . or something regarded as tragic and terminal. By consciously surrendering my entire being to its origins, once a day, am I losing anything? No, I am simply returning for a moment to where I started. I have let go of nothing by my temporary presence in the world of the living.

But that's me. The point is in some way to meditate on death, our own death, often enough that it becomes a real and acceptable part of our lives, rather than something abstract, tragic, and terminal.

I know that facing the real thing, as you are, and truly letting go of everything is hard work, which I am sure makes any meditation a challenge. I so admire you for trying it at this stage of your life, and for remembering that "meditation is not what you think."

Judith's: I love your meditation, and the closing sentiment. But best of all I love the idea of surrender. I can't find much fear of death in me—though tons of fear of pain— or any sense that my own death is in any way tragic. Death of a planet seems tragic, or the death of children or young parents.

Surrendering in the way you describe sounds like a wonderful practice and I'm going to lie down on the floor and try it after you leave this afternoon. What's much harder for me, though, is to surrender to this living body . . . to pain. Although if I accept I can't get anything done and just have to lie on the floor all day, I can sometimes surrender moderately well.

Getting ready for death is hard work, for sure. But I'm finding it interesting to see how much I want to do it (all the parts— from lists, to connecting with people, to meditation, etc.). What I don't like is how on days like today, with fear that anything I do will trigger more pain, I can't do the listed tasks I want or need to do.

"Since I met you, death has become a current in my life," I wrote to her that night, "an almost constant current (and that's a good thing) joining the standard lifetime currents of infancy, family, school, romance, work, marriage, child raising, etc. For this I credit our tiny, spontaneous Death Café . . . and, Judith, I am so grateful for your willingness to join it."

The next morning, I continued the message: "Last night I found myself meditating on death as liberation. Just as sleep liberates us temporarily from consciousness, and all its neuroses, death does so permanently. If one loves life, as we do, then our deaths have to be somewhat tragic. But its inevitability does seem to reduce the tragedy, even give it meaning, and when you think about it in terms of liberation, some beauty as well.

"Knowing too many young people who ended their lives long before they should have, and knowing that some of them were obsessed with death, I truly believe that this current of ours can start way too early in life. For me that's not the case. Nor, given your pain, is it yours. In fact it's the opposite. I'm old and you have a very good reason to let go.

"I now think you were very wise to limit the size of your first Death Café to unscheduled meetings of two members. And I am happy the keep it that way. If you ever want to expand it, and want to include me, I'll stay in. But I'm totally OK with this. Looking forward to seeing you tomorrow, and talking about everything else."

As I said earlier, death meditation is a discipline of mysticism, which, like death itself, is accessible to us all. And so is letting go. And for one mystic to understand the complex, mysterious interior of another, that person must first let go of his own overguarded inwardness. This helped me understand Judith, as she and I cared for each other as only two people without a future can. Being with her forced me into corners of life I might otherwise never have entered. In truth, though, it really wasn't her alone that did this. It was the constant fact that she was about to leave, and even more so that she not only knew she was going to die but exactly how and when.

In true mystic discipline, she had subtracted the greatest of all uncertainties from her life. That constant fact gave her a unique opportunity to lean into death, to talk about it, think about it, meditate on it, and come to see it not only as a teacher and advisor but, as she said more than once, "a friend." The gift she gave me and her beloveds was allowing us to witness her process, and talk openly about it along the way. The impermanence of everything became a central theme of our conversations, and our meditations, as did surrender.

"I'm playing with it, and beginning to feel that I prefer *surrender* to *letting go,*" she said one day, "although I'm not sure yet what the difference is. They do have different energies—letting go a casting off, surrender a sinking in. I'm going to experiment more. Either way, I have to remind myself constantly that life is only borrowed, and we have to give it back . . . the paradox of impermanence."

"Ah, semantics," I fired back, "the curse of wordsmiths. How we torture ourselves in search of 'meaning' and 'understanding' . . . whatever the hell those things mean. Try forgetting the words for a moment, Judith. Stop debating whether surrendering is better than letting go and focus on your resolve to proceed with this . . . without considering the meaning of *resolve.*

I went on . . . perhaps a bit too far.

"You are bound to have second thoughts about everything you are about to do—the date, the time, the method, the necessity, the circumstance, the meaning, the witnesses, and of course you will be troubled throughout by the effect it will have on Sara, and your mother, on Shandy and others who love you, some of whom I imagine wish you weren't going to do this."

I then went overboard: "You know you can change everything. You can postpone, delay, even cancel, and no one will think the less of you. I told you about my friend Matthew, who stopped the process five times before he finally let go. Each time his friends and family who had gathered to watch him leave, and say good-bye, stayed with him and laughed, drank wine, read poetry, and watched grainy home movies about his life. It all added meaning to the experience. And his death was better for the waiting."

And Judith fired back: "Always good to be reminded of my options, Marko, but I'm not considering any of them. None would make anything easier. I do feel the cost of my choices on Sara and others, and I can't even really be sure if what seems like a right action is really right. I know this will cause pain to some, but I've courted paradox all my life, so I can't complain when paradox presents itself now."

That set me to wondering if it was really possible for us to imagine ourselves dead . . . for an individual to think of his own nonbeing . . . to conceive a state of existence where there is no more "I" or "me." Do we deny death simply to give ourselves a false but comforting sense of immortality?

I have known people before who wanted to die, and at times after meeting them, I left thinking it wasn't such a bad idea, for them, and in one case even for the world. But after dozens of Death Café conversations with Judith, and my ever so slow but eventual acceptance of her decision, every time I parted company with her I would be troubled somehow by the sense that she was about to make, if not for herself, for the world, a tragic mistake.

Of course, once I realized her mind was set on the mission, I said nothing to her, or, for that matter, to anyone else. She was, after all, escaping a level of pain I had never experienced (except perhaps for the brief and temporary pain during the passage of a kidney stone), so I couldn't possibly comprehend what she was living through, day and night, in perpetuity.

That said, throughout our friendship I would look for opportunities to subtly question her decision. To the end, there was always part of me that didn't want her to do this, and moments when I'd be tempted to try just once more to talk her out of it. In one meeting in late November, I asked her if any of the other people she had told of her plans had tried to talk her out them. None, she said.

It turned out that wasn't entirely true. Her young niece, Emma, from Minnesota, whom I met a week or so later, a day or two before the end, told me, in front of Judith, that she had at first been completely opposed to the whole idea, and had let her beloved aunt know that in no uncertain terms. "But Judith is headstrong and determined," Emma said, "and I have reluctantly accepted her intentions." I looked at Judith. She smiled and nodded. I knew at that moment that this wasn't the old Judith I was with, the vibrant, poetic, living Judith. This was Judith letting go.

"About the only thing that could change my course," Judith said after that meeting, "is if I found out other people, like you, for example, would be held responsible. Or I suppose if Sara said she needed me to help her through a crisis, I'd postpone. Otherwise, everything that happens, from my decline, to the way loved ones are responding, to rare butterflies flitting around my head as I lay on my daughter's deck, to the light filtering through the trees, confirms my path." I figured if Emma failed, I would fail as well to convince Judith to reconsider her decision, and I never asked again.

CHAPTER 9

Final Days

Death belongs to the dying and those who
love them
—SHERWIN NULAND

During the damp winter days leading up to December 5, I became uneasy, tense, and increasingly sad. I was less productive and noticeably despondent, two unusual states of being for me. One day I could literally feel my heart beginning to break, something I'd never felt before. Two things kept me focused. I still had to meet Judith's daughter, Sara, and her husband, Shandy, then her sister, Debbie, who would be traveling west with her daughter, Emma, Judith's niece, to say goodbye. These would not be easy meetings for any of us, but I looked forward to them both.

I have now met Sara and Shandy twice and hope they will be permanent people in my life. Debbie and Emma I met the last day of Judith's life. More on that in a few pages.

Judith knew I'd been with people as they died, and that I was by then fairly comfortable being in the room, although in all but one other instance, there had been family and friends there as well. I knew that she would eventually tell me whom she wanted at her bedside the last day, if anyone at all.

"Death is a solitary journey," she said. Of course I would have been there if she'd asked me to, but I was so glad she hadn't. I'd already experienced enough misery just thinking about her gone, and was still reeling from a rapid series of untimely deaths that included two children. Watching Judith die would have been more than I could endure.

As the day approached, I began to wonder if she would really go through with it, or delay, or put it off altogether. Then I realized that I was projecting, and that this was something Judith would never do . . . whip Sara and her family around like that. I knew she would postpone if there was good reason to do so, which put me in mind again of her mother, still alive and alert at one hundred, less than two miles from where her daughter would die.

I guess part of me hoped she would at least reschedule back to her birthday in February. But that was not to be. So Wednesday, December 4, Judith; her sister, Debbie; her niece, Emma; her friend Kate; and I met at her place to say farewell. An hour or so after we gathered, Judith asked her sister and niece if she and I could have an hour or so alone. They went for a walk.

Judith and I reminisced about our short and tiny Death Café exchanges, and believe it or not, we laughed a lot. I asked again if I could write our story. And again she said yes. Then, as my allotted hour rolled away, we walked figuratively to the trailhead, hugged, kissed, and said "I love you." I turned away, aching everywhere, and did what I'd been dreading for months: I let Judith go, grateful that she hadn't asked me to return in the morning to watch her die.

*   *   *

Death doesn't come until the dying is over. For Judith, there was really no dying, only pain, constant, untreatable pain hidden from all but her intimates. At noon on December 4, she was as alive and vital as anyone I'd ever known. But unlike most of the people I've known who died unexpectedly in an accident or assassination, or slowly and uncertainly in an ICU, she would be gone in exactly twenty-four hours. For a moment, sudden death seemed preferable.

Watching her process life while navigating her departure from it, I began to see how the shadow of death changes and obscures the meaning of everything, not just life, everything. As she approached her day of departure, I became witness to someone coming in much closer contact with mortality than I ever had, or probably ever would. And watching her process her endgame brought me slowly to within real sight of my own. It was both frightening and exhilarating.

On the way home that afternoon, I began to wonder if it was possible to feel, perhaps even see one's death, even while healthy and completely alive . . . a preview, a trailer from "the Other Side." I lay awake that night and began to look for it. It was hard to make out at first. I had preimagined a sort of indistinct mass of darkness, a pitch-black silent eternity hanging motionless at the center of my being, similar, I imagined, to the "deep black sack" that haunts a dying Ivan Ilyich.* But in the days and nights since, I have redrawn the image, and have begun to realize that death can appear in many forms throughout our entire existence—which, of course, explains the wide variety of graphic images of the Reaper that have appeared since humans who could draw became aware of mortality.

Putting form to death can be a strangely exhilarating experience, even as a mere exercise of imagination. Joan Didion's death images ranged from a "shower of gold" to "an ice island" in the Channel Islands. My own images will change, I'm sure, but right now, while I still see it as an undeniable factor in life, death seems blessedly invisible (factors are rarely visible). As place, as destination, with a little imagination I suspect death can become a better lit and almost visible location somewhere within my being. Even if I'm wrong about any of the images I've conjured up, it won't matter. I won't recall the specific tricks I've played with death in

---

* Leo Tolstoy, *The Death of Ivan Ilyich,* 1886.

its various forms, but until it arrives, I will remember that I enjoyed the games.

When I think about death in those terms, I have to wonder if any being aware of its mortality could possibly live a complete and psychologically healthy life while in denial of death. That seemed to be Judith's defining question. She seemed so sane and settled with her fate that at times I began to believe that terminal illness is, in a strange and macabre way, a perfect gift to someone trying to understand death before it arrives. Paul Kalanithi seems to have seen both his diagnosis and his prognosis that way. "What makes life meaningful enough to go on living?" he asked himself as death approached.

Only when one knows when and how one is going to die, I suppose, can one completely detach one's being from self, or from life itself. Without those certainties, one will always be grasping for something, if only hope. Does that mean that consciousness of mortality gives human life more meaning than nonhuman life? Probably not.

*   *   *

I could help Judith find a method, but only she could find her way. And she did. And allowing me to witness her step-by-step predeath process was her return gift. But the abiding example Judith set, for me and, I believe, for everyone who knew her, was that to her last day on Earth she was living in the very fullest sense of the word. She did recognize that the future was no longer hers; and as she did so, I came to accept the fact that one day it wouldn't be mine, either. But I'm so much better prepared for that reality now, having watched Judith train herself to engage with death, with such deep respect for its certainty that it became part of her, until she gradually let go of everything, and there was nothing but life to release. Hopefully I'll process the close of my own life as sanely and graciously as she closed hers.

For the sake of everyone around me, I so hope I can pull this off, perhaps even leave my grandchildren with the thought that death can be good . . . well, okay . . . and that it really doesn't have to give meaning to life. It just has to be understood as an inexorable part of it, an essential and inseparable element of every living organism, and, if seen through eyes like Judith's, as sacred as the life that precedes it.

As I left her tiny place for the last time, a huge knot of anguish swelling in my heart, Judith handed me another of her intoxicating poems, "Ten to Darkness," the one she said was her best and favorite. It is prophetic, as you'll soon see.

I'd said good-bye to some people I knew were about to die—parents, grandparents, aunts, uncles, and a few close friends. But I'd never given any thought to what I might say to a living friend or loved one if I knew my days were numbered and it was probably the last time I would see them. Judith seemed to have given it a lot of thought.

As I looked at her mobile face for the last time, graced at the moment with that magnetic smile, I began to realize how poets differ from the rest of us. Until that moment, I thought they were just other people who wrote poems. No, poets, at least Judith, Spoon, Kate, and others I've known, are, as Henry James described them, "those on whom nothing is lost." With remarkable attention to detail, they see differently, think differently, regard the world, express themselves, behave, even love a little differently from the rest of us. Because their point of view is unique, what they share with us often seems opaque, downright abstruse at times. But it really isn't so when you consider the source. And here was proof before me, from one who walked her own path and heard things the rest of us didn't hear, who said farewell to a friend forever with an elegiac poem accompanied verbally by a line borrowed from Tom Waits: "Keep your body at home, Marko, and your heart in the wind"—the last words I heard from Judith Tannenbaum.

Driving home in the dark that night, I caught another a glimpse of eternity. Everything I saw out the window seemed impermanent and trivial. I began to understand that letting go of life means so much more than erasing anecdotes, forgiving transgressors, and plucking cards from a Rolodex. It also means dropping one by one all the petty anxieties, hostilities, resentments, and aggravations that burden the living. I didn't know this could happen before death until I watched someone else do it gradually and gracefully during a six-month friendship. All but physical pain became endurable when she knew it was going to end . . . the consolation of death.

When I got home, I read the poem she had given me over and over before going to bed. Here is the last stanza:

> *Darkness, all these nights I've heard you in*
> *   the wind.*
> *I've felt your calling, but have turned away,*
> *curled my body round itself,*
> *rocked myself toward sleep.*
> *Now your fingers chant against my skin*
> *and though I cannot see your face*
> *I open to your rising.*
> *You sing silent songs in my ear and I*
> *   welcome you deep inside me.*
> *There is nothing that I know*
> *as I let you move me through the night*
> *but even now I feel a stirring . . .*

Of course I had trouble sleeping. As I tossed through the night, uneasy and brokenhearted, I recalled and repeated a sentence from Paul Kalanithi: "The time comes to many when they must ask themselves what makes their life worth living." That became Judith's abiding question, and now it was mine.

Then I thought about another question, this one raised by Dimitri Shostakovich: Do we create art in defiance of death . . . as some kind of protection against mortality? The brilliant composer, who believed that fear of death was the deepest of all human emotions, seemed to think so. "The irony lies in the fact that under the influence of that fear people create poetry, prose, and music," he wrote. Through their art "they try to strengthen their ties with the living."

I turned on my bedside light, opened a journal I'd been keeping throughout our friendship, and remained mute. I had nothing to add.

The following morning, a powerful storm moved in. But I was determined to do what I had earlier told Judith I would do the day she let go. "I will go somewhere sacred and think of you all day," I told her, to which she responded, "I love to think of you somewhere sacred on December fifth. That will help me let go and move on. Thanks so much for telling me."

*   *   *

I am a storm walker. It's difficult to keep me indoors when there is wind, rain, and thunder outside, better yet an icy blizzard. I thrill at the memory of standing on the bluffs at Aberdaron, in Wales, feeling the full force of the constant tempest that only comes off the Irish Sea. As a young working cowboy in Wyoming, I loved riding directly into dust storms. And I'll never forget wandering the long western shore of Haida Gwaii as a North Pacific typhoon tossed thirty- foot driftwood logs thundering against the cliffs below me.

So that morning of December 5, I climbed up Olema Ridge, a steep, sloping meadow four miles south of my home, and walked face-first into a ferocious rain-whipped gale. And during the time I knew she would be inhaling her nitrogen,* I wailed "Judith" into the storm. It was the only way I could let her go.

I felt like that proverbial leaf at the mercy of the wind, my only lasting hope being that none of my neighbors saw or heard me, or, if they did, they knew in advance that many psychotherapists and other soul healers regard grief as a mental illness,

---

* Nitrogen would not kill her. It's not toxic. In fact, it is 78 percent of the air we breathe. It would be a complete lack of oxygen that would render her unconscious in about forty seconds and gone forever in less than six minutes.

temporary perhaps, but nonetheless a form of madness. "Pathological bereavement," one called it in an open debate over whether to regard grief as a normal human process or a mental disorder in *DSM-V*.* I prefer "momentary madness."

A day or two later I realized that most of the rage I felt that morning had been aimed at my new friend, wise advisor, and secret teacher—Death. By then I should have known better.

---

* During revisions made by the American Psychiatric Association between the fourth and fifth editions of their *Diagnostic and Statistical Manual of Mental Disorders* (DSM) the question was raised as to whether grief is a normal human process or a mental disorder that requires diagnosis and treatment. *DSM-IV* said probably not; *DSM-V*, the manual under current use, says yes, the depression that accompanies grief is no different from any other clinical depression, and should be treated as such.

A Death of One's Own

Love and death are the great gifts
that are given to us;
mostly they are passed on unopened.
—RAINER MARIA RILKE

Part of grieving is not wanting to let go of feelings we had for someone when that person was alive. Despite our efforts to hold on, those feelings subside, of course, drifting gradually into the background. And our sadness comes from watching that happen, as grief works at it its own pace, which, of course, is different for everyone, in every situation, and with every death.

Unlike the story itself, that part of the process, the lethal bereavement, never seems to end. Nor does the love felt for the departed. In fact, it becomes the driving force of our lasting grief, and ultimately, it seems, a companion of death itself.

Having lived a long life among many friends and relatives, who have since died, I've watched more than a few approach the end overwhelmed with tears, panic, longing, and a refusal to let go of anything. Some pleaded for mercy, others whined about the length of their unfinished bucket list, and many saw some sort of injustice in their fate. So it was refreshing to watch someone dive boldly into her final day without a single regret, while refusing to the very last hour to say that she was dying.

Of course she was both right and wrong about that. By one definition, we are all dying ... always. Aware of the semantic ambiguity of the word *dying*, Judith believed that we are all living full-time until the true dying starts. And her true dying, she believed, wouldn't start until she took that first breath of nitrogen. Semantic subterfuge? Perhaps. I saw it as unshakable composure.

After Judith left, I literally dove, though perhaps not quite so boldly, into death, which I realized by then had, as a subject, been shoved, by me and by Western civilization, into the sterile seclusion of nursing homes, intensive care units, and other places people are sent to die out of sight. While I had lost friends and relatives, and been with dying people to the end, I really hadn't thought that much about death itself before I met and grew close to Judith. While grieving her absence, I began reading everything I could to learn about where she might be.*

---

* It began with the classics: Lucretius, Epicurus, Montaigne, Nietzsche, Camus, Heidegger, Ariès, Sartre, Dostoyevsky. Then I moved on to the thanatologists—principally Elisabeth Kübler-Ross, Stephen Levine, Sogyal Rinpoche, and Sherwin Nuland. And finally some modern classics: Mitch Albom's *Tuesdays with Morrie,* Atul Gawande's *Being Mortal,* Christopher Hitchens's *Mortality,* Ernest Becker's *The Denial of Death,* Stephen Jamison's *Final Acts of Love,* Frank Ostaseski's *The Five Invitations,* Michael Hebb's delightful but somewhat schmaltzy *Let's Talk about Death (over Dinner),* Carlos Castaneda's *TheTeachings of Don Juan,* and, once again, Paul Kalanithi's heart-stopper, *When Breath Becomes Air,* all with hopes I would understand what I had been going through the past six months as I watched someone subtract one of the great uncertainties from her life and learn more about the fate we all face, and how her lesson fit the various ways Western philosophers, Eastern mystics, and deep thinkers from other cultures have described and dealt with it.

Reading too much about death, one comes away with a lot of sophistry, and many more questions than answers. Of course, questions are the lifeblood of philosophic inquiry (and journalism), and sometimes the best we can hope for from philosophers grappling with a difficult subject are more questions, such as the following.

- Can one be completely happy while fearing death?
- Can life or death be understood alone, absent the other?
- Is fearing death simply fearing nonexistence?
- Does death give life a sense of urgency it would otherwise lack?
- How much easier it is to imagine the death of another than it is of our own? And which death should I fear the most, that person's or mine?
- Is the experience of dying in any way the experience of death, or merely the final experience of a fading life?

- Is it easier while living to conceive of existence before birth or after death? Or are they really the same thing?
- Can one be a spectator of death while being dead?
- Do people who are overattached to their own personality, as some analysts claim, really have the most trouble dying?
- Is my death generically different from anyone else's?
- Is death deterministic?
- If so, and it's inevitable, and followed by nothing, why bother doing anything?
- Is nothingness preferable to suffering?

Occasionally I stroll slowly through those questions, waiting a minute or two between each of them, with hopes of learning something from an answer. Aside from being left with a bunch of metaphysical quandaries, many of which can really be understood or solved only through contemplative practice, I really didn't learn much of importance from the process, or from philosophers, pundits, or journalists, that my all too short friendship with Judith hadn't already taught me. And I truly don't think I need to know more than I learned in our six months together to finish this blessedly long life I've been given and accept its denouement with the grace and equanimity I witnessed as Judith let go. But I am still left with questions of my own:

- Do the dark and silent eternities on either side of birth and death both give meaning to life . . . and to time?
- If we don't fear and despise the first spell of darkness, does it make sense to fear and despise the second?

(The difference, of course, between the abyss that exists before life and the abyss that comes after it is that during the first abyss nobody misses you.)

- If there were no beginning or end to life, would time not become unlimited and essentially meaningless?
- When someone close to us dies, do we all wonder about that person's very last moment alive, or is it just me who envisions the oncoming truck, feels the

sudden chest pain, follows the bullet through the brain, the terrorist's blade, the lungful of nitrogen, all leading up or down to a slow, or fast, descent into silence?

- Does anyone else wonder if the light we hear so much about at the end is a vision of a higher power, or simply the last light of life, which will soon burn out and fade to eternal darkness?

So many mysteries.

It seems to be easier to explore and grasp the meaning of something when it's heard in our own language. I learned this at a young age. Though I am now a roaring agnostic, I was raised a High Church Anglican. As a boy growing up in Canada, many of the Masses I attended were in Latin, as were some religious ceremonies, even funerals.

So when I heard a graveside vicar chant *"Media vita in morte sumus,"* I knew what he was saying: "In the midst of life we are in death." But because it was in Latin, and I don't think, or dream, in Latin, I didn't really think much about what I was hearing.

During my six months with Judith, death was pretty much all I thought about, and I'm beginning to grasp its very direct and simple meaning. It is always with us. I am living in my corpse.

Judith grew to understand, even love those realities. I'm working on them as I watch life and death merge into that greatest of all mysteries.

*   *   *

One of my readers, Doris Ober, had recently lost her husband. She told me after reading a draft of this book that it made her aware that she and Richard had somehow missed out on this conversation. "Yes, we talked about his dying and what needed to be done. But we never talked about death itself." She said she could see how my friendship with Judith had changed me.

I try to remember myself before I met Judith. I doubt anyone else would notice a difference, but the changes in me are very real and large. However, they are internal, personal, mostly spiritual, invisible, and almost impossible to describe, particularly by someone who breaks out in hives while writing in the first person. So I think I'll leave them be and close by simply saying:

Thank you Judith.

Whenever the wind roars through the redwoods, I'll remember you. And having known you, I'll never be the same. Something new has emerged within me as I've gradually awakened, thanks to your example, from the all too comfortable habit of avoidance. As I told you near the end, "This was not something I sought out. It happened . . . a beautiful synchronicity, with which very few of us are ever blessed." And rarely does synchronicity work out this well.

We have been student and teacher to each other, Judith, teacher and student. I have to confess that I felt helpless at times, at both roles. And no one likes to feel helpless in the face of another's affliction, particularly when it's so threatening. As guide, friend, and facilitator, we need to feel in control. And at times, I have to confess, I was losing control, not of you, but of myself, and my sanity. Then, even as you fought pain and confronted death, you put me back on track.

I may not be completely prepared, Judith, but much better now than before we met. I also feel kinder for having watched you with friends and family, wiser for having heard your thoughts, more poetic and wide open to new ways of seeing, simply for having been in your presence for six all too short months. And as Wendy told you about what was happening to me when you were still alive, my heart was being opened . . . by you, of course. You also taught me how to let go—not on death's terms, but on your own. For that alone, I will never forget and will always love you.

Yes, it was idyllic, but I like to believe that somewhere in our lives we all deserve one perfect, innocent, grace-filled friendship, and this was mine. And for it my thanks are boundless.

And, and as I promised you, never again will I take life for granted.

If this friendship had to close the way it did, I just wish it had happened when I was younger and

Judith was older. Judith was simply too young to die, and I would be so much better prepared for old age, and death, had I experienced this encounter earlier in life. That in no way diminishes my admiration for the way she died, or my gratitude for the lesson she gave me on the fine art of leaving life gracefully . . . by simply letting go.

ABOUT THE AUTHOR

MARK DOWIE, an investigative historian, retired recently from the University of California Berkeley Graduate School of Journalism, where he taught science, environmental reporting, and foreign correspondence. In his final year there, he conducted a series of courses on the environment in China. Previously, he was editor-at-large of InterNation, a transnational feature syndicate based in Paris, and before that a publisher and editor of *Mother Jones* magazine.

He lives on a cattle station south of Willow Point, California.

Printed in the USA
CPSIA information can be obtained
at www.ICGtesting.com
JSHW061403190424
61517JS00010B/202

9 781613 322352